PROJECT PANDA WATCH

PROJECT PANDA WATCH

MIRIAM SCHLEIN

illustrated by Robert Shetterly

and with photographs

ATHENEUM

NEW YORK

1984

PHOTO CREDITS

Chicago Tribune *and Brookfield Zoo 40*
National Zoo 75
New York Zoological Society 42, 47

LIBRARY OF CONGRESS CATALOGING IN PUBLICATION DATA

Schlein, Miriam.
Project panda watch.

SUMMARY: Discusses a project which attempts to
provide food for giant pandas during critical bamboo
emergencies, periods when their only natural food dies
off during one phase of its growth cycle.
1. Giant panda—Juvenile literature. 2. Wildlife
conservation—Juvenile literature. [1. Giant panda.
2. Wildlife conservation] I. Shetterly, Robert, ill.
II. Title.
QL737.C214S35   1984   639.9'7974443   84-2914
ISBN 0-689-31071-4

Text copyright © 1984 by Miriam Schlein
Pictures copyright © 1984 by Robert Shetterly
Published simultaneously in Canada by
McClelland & Stewart, Ltd.
Composition by Maryland Linotype Corporation,
Baltimore, Maryland
Printed and bound by Fairfield Graphics,
Fairfield, Pennsylvania
Designed by Judith Lerner
First Edition

CONTENTS

PROJECT PANDA WATCH

PIKA

The tents are high in the mountains.

ONE

A PANDA IS CAPTURED

THE TENT is set in a clearing, high in the mountains. It is large and solid-looking and it seems as if it's been there for a while. Smoke is coming out through a roof pipe. Nearby, a stack of firewood is piled up.

Suddenly the silence is broken as a man comes running down the mountainside. He is shouting excitedly, half in Chinese, half in English, *"Bei-shung! Bei-shung!* Good news! We have finally caught one!"

Three men rush out of the tent and listen as the runner explains things and points upward. Then they go back inside, and quickly gather up some special equipment. In a few minutes, they are following the runner back up the mountainside.

Bei-shung is the Chinese word for panda. Who are these men, and why are they trying to catch a panda?

Hu Jin Chu is a wildlife expert—a teacher of zoology,

3

and one of China's finest naturalists. George Schaller has come from the United States, where he is Director of ARC (Animal Research and Conservation) at the Bronx Zoo in New York. He is known worldwide for his work in learning about different animals by observing them in the wild. Howard Quigley is an expert in radiotelemetry —also from the Bronx Zoo. They are part of the first research team ever to study pandas in the wild.

It's not going to be easy. Since pandas live hidden in the dense bamboo forest, it would be impossible to watch the pandas and learn about them in that way. So, they are going to "observe" them in a different way. What they are planning to do with the captured panda is put a radio collar around its neck, then set it free. Signals from the collar will help them to track its movements and to know what it is doing without their actually seeing it.

That is why, for about a month now, they had been trying to capture a panda. They had traps out on the mountainside—not the kind that would hurt an animal, but large metal cages, covered with logs as camouflage, and baited with a piece of meat hanging inside. If the meat were touched, a catch would be released, the door slammed shut, and the panda trapped inside.

Every day they checked the traps—but had no luck; they were always empty. One day they *almost* caught one. When they went to check a trap, they saw a panda not in it, but walking around it, trying to figure out how to get at the bait hanging inside. A bird had set off the trigger mechanism, causing the door to slam shut, and the panda could not get in.

But today, their luck seems to have changed. They have been climbing upward now for more than an hour. It's not easy walking; the slopes are steep, but they push onward eagerly. Often they have to climb up and around outcroppings of rock. Several times they cross streams by walking on logs that have fallen across them.

Finally they reach the trap. The good news is true. There, inside it, is their first panda. They stand for a few minutes, catching their breath after the long climb. Then they get to work.

The first thing they have to do is tranquilize the panda. This is not as easy as it sounds, even though the animal is in a cage. Pandas have huge jaws and teeth, so it is not a great idea to just stick your hand into the cage. Also, you don't want to jab the panda in a vein or a nerve, where it may be harmful. It's best to aim for a shoulder muscle.

Howard Quigley prepares the hypodermic needle. Then he waits for the right moment. The panda is moving around. Finally, Quigley sees his chance. He jumps forward and gives the panda a fast jab in the shoulder. Then they all watch and wait.

The panda seems to be getting groggy. Its big head begins to nod. In about ten minutes it is sprawled out on its back in a deep sleep.

They open the cage door and pull the panda out. First, they put the radio collar on its neck. They do this carefully. Too tight, and it would be uncomfortable for the

panda. Too loose, and it might fall off or get snagged in the thickets. When it's fitted, Howard Quigley checks to see that it gives out signals. It does.

Then, working quickly, they get all the information they can about the panda. They measure, weigh and examine it. She is a female and weighs 190 pounds (86 kilograms). Her teeth are yellowish and a bit worn down. Some of them are missing. They judge from all this that she is at least twelve years old.

They do everything at top speed, because they know the tranquilizer will only last about fifteen minutes. They don't want to be peering into the panda's mouth when she wakes up.

When they finish, they drag her back into the trap, then wait. Soon she shakes her head and staggers to her feet. Standing on top of the trap, safely out of her way, they lift the door. They watch as she comes out of the trap and walks off. In a minute or two, they can no longer see her; she has disappeared into the bamboo thicket.

They decide to name the panda Zhen-Zhen. This means "rare treasure" or "precious" in Chinese. As they watch her walk off, they know that Project Panda Watch has really begun.

When the two pandas, Ling-Ling and Hsing-Hsing, arrived at the National Zoo in Washington, D.C. in 1972, crowds came to see them. People loved watching the roly-poly cubs as they tumbled around, turned somersaults, balanced on barrels and played with balls. No one taught the pandas these things—they just seemed to like to do them. And they were certainly fun to watch.

But how do pandas act and what do they do when they're not in a zoo? The truth is, scientists knew very little about panda behavior in the wild.

Because pandas live hidden in the bamboo forests, it had always been difficult to learn much about them. In fact, there was more that we did *not* know than we did know.

We knew that pandas ate bamboo. But how much do

they eat? How often do they eat? How far do pandas roam? Are they active in the daytime or, like many animals, are they active in the night and sleep through the day? Pandas resemble bears. Do they live in a cave or some other sort of den, as bears do? It is cold where they live. Do they hibernate in winter, the way bears do?

Nobody knew. These were some of the things that Project Panda Watch hoped to find out.

People loved to watch the playful panda cubs.

TWO

THE LAND OF THE PANDAS

IT WAS THE WINTER of 1980-81 when George Schaller went to China to join Hu Jin Chu in the project. He flew in to the city of Chengdu, in the Szechuan Province. From there he traveled by van to the Wolong Natural Reserve. Pandas live high in the Himalaya Mountains, at elevations of 7,000 to 11,000 feet (2,133 to 3,352 meters) above sea level. This is an isolated part of the world where no one lives and very few people have seen. So the rest of Schaller's journey had to be made on foot, climbing mountain trails.

George Schaller's wife, Kay, went with him. Everything they needed—scientific equipment, food, clothing, pots, medical supplies—had to be carried up from this point on. They carried some of their things in backpacks; porters carried the rest. The base camp is in panda territory, 8,300 feet (2,530 meters) above sea level. It takes two days' climbing to reach it.

It is a wild place, yet peaceful, up there where the pandas live. Tall spruce and fir trees tower above the bamboo. The terrain is rocky and steep, leading up to even higher peaks above. Mountain streams and water-falls splash over the rocks. It is so high up that clouds drift through the trees.

Some birds are seen. Woodpeckers clatter high up on tree trunks. Ground-living purple pheasants are seen walking about. Flying overhead are large groups of snow pigeons. Small mammals—mice and voles and shrews—run through the undergrowth, and little whistling pikas called "mouse-hares," that look like guinea pigs, live among the rocks.

It is one of the last truly wild areas in the world, and many unusual animals live here as well. On the higher peaks are climbers, such as the goatlike gorals, and furry, chunky takins and the smaller, sure-footed serows. In the bamboo forests there are small delicate muntjacs, or "barking deer." Roaming about there are also meat-eating predators; leopards and wild dogs. And high in the trees swing groups of golden monkeys. Like the panda, this is the only place in the world where they are found.

Before Zhen-Zhen was captured, Schaller and Hu went out each day to do preliminary work. They wanted to learn everything they could about the panda's habitat. And—with luck—maybe they would even see a panda. Climbing about on the steep terrain, they looked for signs of the animals.

It is bitter cold. The thermometer outside their tent reads 14° Fahrenheit (−10° Celsius). And up on the ex-

GOLDEN
MONKEY

SEROW

DENDROCOPUS
WOOD
PECKER

MUNTJAC

TAKIN

BLOOD
PLEASANT

posed slopes, it is even colder. There has been no snow yet; it is very late this year. That makes their job even harder, because pandas would leave footprints in the snow. But they do see other things. A clump of broken-off bamboo stalks shows them a panda has stopped in that spot to eat. Sometimes they see a rounded pressed-down spot where a panda has lain down to rest. They know it was a panda because there are panda droppings nearby. Pandas make very large and frequent droppings; they are easy to recognize.

Signs like this that an animal has passed by are called the animal's "spoor." Pandas are around; there is no doubt about it. But a month has gone by, and they still have not seen one.

Heavy snow finally begins to fall. Searching about the slopes, Hu and Schaller begin to see some panda prints. Hu Jin Chu carefully traces the prints on plastic. A footprint is as individual as a fingerprint. They save and compare them. They know there are at least several pandas in the area. But still, they have had no sight of one.

The bamboo stays green through the winter, even when there is snow on the ground. And many of the trees growing high above the bamboo are evergreens—fir and spruce and hemlocks. These remain green too. The panda's black and white bodies blend in with the snow and the dark shadows of the bamboo forest around them. It is possible to pass very close to a panda and not be aware it is there. There are signs of them all around—

Footprints are as individual as fingerprints.

Two pandas are tracked and sighted in a tree.

but where are the animals themselves? Perhaps there are a very few in the area.

Then early one morning they see panda tracks in the snow; two sets, about 100 feet (30 meters) from their camp. They are new, fresh tracks.

They follow the tracks for most of the day. Finally, up in a tall spruce tree, some 40 feet (12 meters) from the ground, they see a small panda. On one of the thicker lower limbs sits a larger panda. The little one gives a long howl. Then the two pandas just sit there for a while. The large one seems to have been chasing the small one. Schaller and Hu do not know why. After a while, the big panda shimmies down the tree rump first and disappears into the bamboo thicket. Mist begins to drift through the air. The small panda seems to be set for the night, up on his perch. Hu and Schaller are pleased as they head back toward the base camp. At last they have seen—actually *seen*—some pandas!

THREE

PANDAS AND BAMBOO

PANDAS DID NOT always live high on these mountain slopes. A million years ago, they lived in many lower parts of China. We know this from fossils that have been found. Even a few thousand years ago, pandas still roamed over large parts of eastern China.

Two events forced the pandas to move into their present habitat. Both had to do with bamboo.

First, the climate began to get drier in the lower areas of China. Since bamboo grows best in damp places, it did not thrive in the lowlands any more. And you cannot separate pandas from bamboo. It is what they eat. So, pandas began to move up into more mountainous areas, where it was misty and damp, and bamboo still grew.

Then, in more recent times, more and more land was cleared to make way for cities and villages and farms. As the bamboo forests on the lower mountain slopes were cut down, the pandas were forced to move higher and

USSR

WOLOONG RESERVE

SZECHUAN
PROVINCE

NEPAL

CURRENT RANGE

PREVIOUS RANGE

INDIA

PAKISTAN

BURMA

LAOS

THAILAND

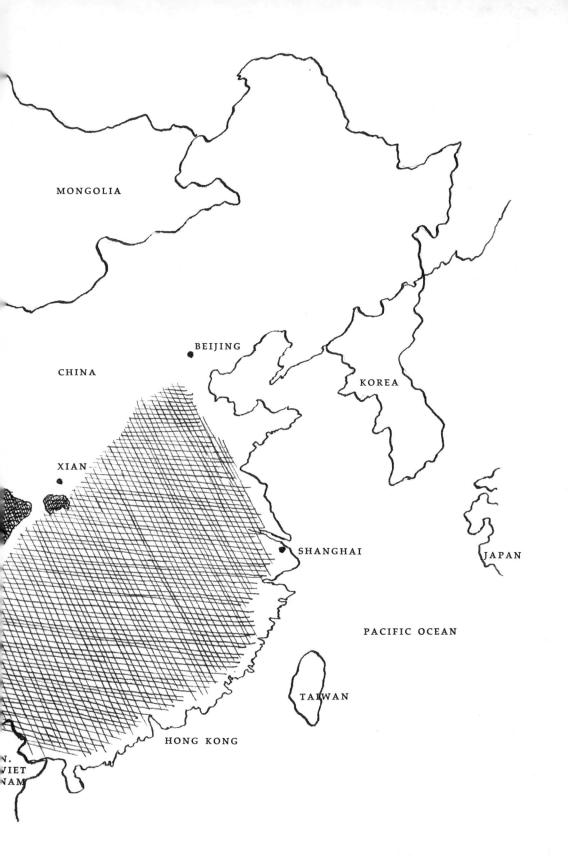

higher up into the mountains, where large bamboo forests still existed. Now it is the only place they can survive. Up there, on those high slopes, they are surrounded by their food supply.

Pandas can eat other things. In fact, they love meat. Sometimes they catch and eat a small animal—a mouse, a vole, a pika. But pandas are too slow-moving and clumsy to be able to get much food this way. Besides, there is not much small game up there for them to catch. They sometimes also eat crocuses, iris, gentians and tufted grass. But the bamboo is their main food. Without it, they could not live.

Bamboo is a kind of giant grass, but it's very different from the grass we see. It has a thick, round, woodlike hollow stalk, or stem. Though there are many different types of bamboo, some growing to heights of 100 feet, the bamboo in panda territory grows 10 to 12 feet high (about 3 to 3½ meters).

The woodlike stalk of the bamboo, called the "culm," is about 1½ inches (3.8 centimeters) thick. This is what the pandas eat.

Sitting on their rumps in a relaxed position, they grasp a stalk, pull it downward, and with their big teeth, snap it off at the bottom. Holding the stalk in their front paws, they bring it up to their mouth. With a fast twist of the head, they strip off the tough outer part of the stalk. Then, still holding it, they munch on it starting from one end. It takes them about 40 seconds to finish a stalk. Then they start on the next one.

A panda can pick up its food because there is some-

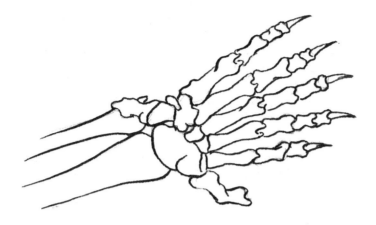

thing special about its paws. It has a "sixth finger," sometimes called a false thumb. It's not really a finger. It's part of the wristbone that sticks out about 1½ inches (3.3 centimeters) from the wrist and is covered by tough flesh. The panda uses this false thumb the way we use our thumbs—to grasp things.

In other ways, too, the panda's body is well equipped for its bamboo diet. It has powerful jaws and large, ridged teeth that can easily crunch through the hard bamboo stalk. Its esophagus—the tube leading down to its stomach—has a thick, tough lining, so it is not punctured by the splintery bamboo as it goes down. The panda's stomach wall, too, is tough and muscular.

After Zhen-Zhen was collared and released, she remained hidden in the bamboo thickets, and the research team did not see her again for several months. But now they are not only aware of where she is, but what she is doing. The "beep-beep-beep" of her radio collar tells them that.

When the beeps are more frequent, they know she is moving around. When the signals are slow and far apart, they know she is sleeping. Through Zhen-Zhen, they begin to learn a lot about panda habits that no one had ever known.

Pandas spend ten to sixteen hours or more of every day eating, moving slowly through the forest, snapping and crunching on the bamboo. When they are tired, they rest or sleep for one to four hours, or even a shorter time, just where they are. They sometimes will rest for a while in a hollow tree or under a ledge. Then they go on their way.

For five days of every month, Zhen-Zhen's movements are charted for a twenty-four-hour period. That's how the scientists know her wandering goes on night and day.

Though Zhen-Zhen keeps on wandering, she doesn't really go very far. She doesn't have to—she is surrounded by her food, always. Some days she travels only 600 feet (about 183 meters). That is the same as about two short city blocks. At that rate, in eight days she will wander less than one mile.

Schaller and Hu are astounded by the amount that Zhen-Zhen eats. Following her trail by the beeps of her collar, they find that she stops to eat every few minutes.

They don't follow too closely; they don't want to scare

her, but every time they find a clump of broken-off bamboo stems, they know she has stopped to eat. It is spring now and she is eating young bamboo shoots. By counting the stems they estimate that Zhen-Zhen may eat about six hundred of these a day. This means she may eat about one quarter of a million bamboo stalks every year.

By weighing some bamboo stalks, the scientists calculate that a panda may eat about 66 pounds (30 kilograms) or more of food per day. Since Zhen-Zhen weighs 190 pounds (87 kilograms), this is about one-third of Zhen-Zhen's body weight. (If you weigh 100 pounds, it would be comparable to your eating 33 pounds of food a day.) Sixty-six pounds a day comes to almost 25,000 pounds (about 11,325 kilograms) of food each year!

Why do pandas eat so much?

They have to, because of the kind of intestines—or guts—that they have.

Even though pandas live almost totally on bamboo, since they do eat some meat—though not much—this technically makes them the kind of animal we call a carnivore—a meat eater. And pandas have the same kind of gut (the passageway in which the food goes through their system) that meat eaters have—a very short gut.

Since meat, as it passes through the system, does not take much time to be digested, a short gut works fine for most carnivores. But vegetation, like grass, leaves, or bamboo, needs more time to be digested. That is why herbivores—animals who eat vegetation—normally have longer guts.

Locating Zhen-Zhen's position by radio equipment.

So the panda really has a diet of vegetation, but the wrong kind of gut to digest it properly. The bamboo passes through the panda's short gut so quickly, it does not have enough time to be properly digested; that is, to be changed and broken up into different substances and absorbed into the body to give it nourishment. So the pandas' bodies do not benefit from most of what they eat. A lot of the bamboo a panda eats just comes out in its droppings, undigested.

This is why pandas must eat such an enormous amount. They are forced to keep eating almost constantly, just to get enough nourishment to stay alive .

Possibly the panda is in this short-gut predicament because it may be descended from some ancestor of the past whose diet was mostly meat, and its intestines simply did not evolve or change as the diet changed.

FOUR

PANDAS ALONE,
YET TOGETHER

IN THE SPRING, heavy rains begin. The forest is a dripping world of green. Everything is more colorful. Wild primroses bloom, and rhododendrons grow all over the mountainsides, making spots of purple, pink, red and yellow. More birds appear, and the golden monkeys swing through the trees in larger troops than before—sometimes 300 of them together.

By now, Project Panda Watch has collared two more pandas. One is a small young male, weighing 120 pounds (about 54 kilograms). By his weight, and by examining his teeth, they figure he is two or three years old. They name him Long-Long, meaning Dragon.

Because Long-Long is young and still growing, they must be especially careful in fitting his radio collar. It should not fit him exactly, because as he grows and his neck gets bigger, they don't want the collar to get too tight and choke him. It should not be too loose, either; it could get caught on something and trap him, or it could fall off. They fit it on him carefully, and let him go.

The third panda they catch is a female. Like Long-Long, she is young and not fully grown. She is examined, fitted and released. They name her Ning-Ning, meaning "kind and peaceful."

One morning George Schaller leaves the tent and walks about the mountainside. On a high ridge, he stops to put together the antenna he carries and tunes in to Zhen-Zhen's frequency. Her signals come in loud and clear. She must be very close. He sits down at the edge of a small clearing. Suddenly, from within the bamboo thicket, he hears a snap, then a crunching sound. Schaller peers in. First he sees nothing; it is dark in the thicket. Then he sees a shadowy movement, and he makes out Zhen-Zhen's form. She is sitting, legs stretched out in front. She leans forward, grasps a bamboo shoot, and snaps it off with her teeth. Then the crunching begins again. She is eating the young bamboo shoots that grow in the spring. They are more tender and tasty than the old stalks. In less than a minute she finishes one and grabs another.

Schaller watches and takes pictures. Suddenly, Zhen-Zhen lifts her nose. She seems to sense him, but she does not rush deeper into the bamboo thicket. Instead, oddly enough, she comes right into the clearing. For the first time since the day she was in the trap, Schaller sees her—her black-circled eyes, her small pom-pom ears. She approaches to about 35 feet (9 meters) from Schaller stares at him, then turns and slowly goes back into the bamboo. She sits down close to the edge and makes a soft bleating

Why do pandas eat so much?

sound. Then, to Schaller's surprise, she dozes off. In a few minutes she wakes up and walks deeper into the bamboo.

George Schaller has had an experience few people have ever had—seeing a panda face to face, free, in its own habitat. During the two months she was collared, although they had learned a lot about her habits, they had not seen her once. No wonder the panda and the life it leads has always been a mystery.

The study area for Project Panda Watch is small. It is nine square miles (about 23 square kilometers). Only seven pandas live in it.* Sometimes a few others wander in for a while, then leave. Project Panda Watch is soon tracking five of these pandas by radio collar.

Although pandas wander all the time, they do not wander very far. Each panda stays in its own small part of the bamboo forest. This is called its "range." In a

* This is comparable to about 18 pandas living on the island of Manhattan (22.3 square miles, where about one-and-a-half million people live.)

whole year, Zhen-Zhen never leaves her small range of 1½ square miles (about 4 square kilometers).

The pandas' ranges all overlap somewhat, so a panda will often wander into a neighboring range, stay awhile, then wander back out.

Although pandas wander alone, they are aware that other pandas are there. They leave "signs" for each other. Standing on their hind legs, they will scratch bark from part of a tree. They may do this to sharpen their claws, or they may do it to show that they have been by here.

They may leave signs in other ways, too. Pandas have special scent glands on their backsides. Zoo pandas rub their backsides against special hard surfaces of their enclosures, leaving a sticky secretion that has their own personal scent. Male pandas also urinate on vertical surfaces while standing on their front paws in handstand position.

In the wild, they could give and receive valuable information in this way. By a scent left on some hard surface—say, a tree—another panda coming by could tell how long ago the first panda was there and whether it was a male or female. The scent could also show whether the panda was in rut—ready to mate. This information is especially important in the mating season.

Deer, wolves and many other animals leave messages for each other in this way. It is called "scent marking."

FIVE

THE BABY PANDA

LATER IN the spring, Zhen-Zhen seems to be getting very restless. The signals from her collar are coming in very fast beeps. This means she is moving around much more than usual.

Zhen-Zhen is not the only one acting differently. It is the mating season. Male pandas are so restless that some of them are biting down small trees. The forest is not the quiet place it used to be. All around them, Hu, Schaller and the others hear barking, mooing and yipping. The male pandas, who are so solitary and quiet the rest of the year, are now saying: "Here I am, I am a male panda, and I'm ready for mating!"

The females have also gotten noisy and have suddenly begun to bleat a lot. Now, for the second time, George Schaller sees Zhen-Zhen. She is walking, head down, going faster than the usual casual panda walk, up a trail. She passes close to Schaller, but pays no attention to him.

Following her a minute later is a male panda. Then a second male shows up. They both want to mate with Zhen-Zhen. But the first male is older, larger and stronger. He chases the other one away. Then he and Zhen-Zhen mate.

They stay together for a day or so. During this time, they mate a number of times. Then they separate, each returning once more to solitary wandering.

Maybe Zhen-Zhen will give birth to a baby panda. Maybe not.

Baby pandas are born four or five months after the mating of their parents. As the time of birth approaches, the female no longer wanders so much. She finds a cave-like spot under an overhanging rock ledge or a big, hollow fir tree. Here, in this protected place, in late August or early September, is where her baby is born.

The baby panda is unusually tiny. It weighs only about 4 ounces (112 grams). Since the mother probably weighs about 200 pounds (90 kilograms), this means the panda mother is about 800 times heavier than her baby. That is an astonishing difference in size. Most mammal babies are much closer in size to their mothers. (Human babies often weigh about 7 pounds—about 3½ kilograms. If a human mother with a 7 pound baby were 800 times heavier than her baby, she would weigh almost 5,600 pounds. That's nearly three tons!)

The baby panda looks nothing like a grown-up panda. It has pink skin, with a few white hairs. Its eyes are closed, it has no teeth and it cannot crawl. Very gently,

Gently the mother picks up the baby with her mouth.

the mother picks it up with her mouth, and places the baby on her breast, so it can drink her milk.

She leans against the back of the cave or tree hollow and cradles her baby in her paws. She licks it to clean it. The baby, though tiny, has a loud cry.

In a week's time, black fur begins to grow on its ears, shoulders and around its eyes. After a month, its eyes are still not open. But the baby panda grows quickly. In three months it weighs about 12 pounds (about 5.5 kilograms) and is two feet long (about 61 centimeters). It can crawl now, and has started to get its teeth. At six months, it begins to eat bamboo.

The young panda stays with its mother for about a year and a half. Then it leaves to begin its own wandering, alone in the bamboo forest.

The baby panda is born in a hollow tree.

SIX

THE FIRST PANDA
IN THE UNITED STATES

IN THE YEAR 685, the emperor of China sent the ruler of Japan "two living white bears, and 70 white bear skins."

The Chinese name for panda is bei-shung—which means "white bear." Were those ancient "white bears" pandas? We don't know. We cannot be sure. Some people think they may have been polar bears, caught by Chinese hunters from the north.

To the Chinese, the panda has always been a rare treasure. It was felt that this shy and mysterious creature, living high above in the mist and the snow, was a sort of godlike creature. Few people ever saw one. Sometimes a panda might come down and try to get honey from villagers' beehives. Otherwise, they were seldom seen.

The panda was not known to the Western world until 1879, when it was discovered by Père Armand David, a French missionary in China. He was traveling deep in

the interior of China, where few Westerners had ever gone. There, some men showed him the body of a panda. (They had caught it alive, but had killed it because it was easier to carry that way.)

Looking at it, Père David knew immediately that this was a species of animal the Western world did not know about. Excited by his discovery, he sent news of this "new" animal to natural scientists in Paris.

These were the days of the big game hunter. When they heard of this new, interesting animal, what they wanted was the thrill of personally shooting one. Expeditions from the United States and Europe soon set out to China to hunt for panda. They plunged through the thickets with guides and hunting dogs. But for a long time, none of them even *saw* a panda.

Then, in 1928, two Americans, Kermit and Theodore Roosevelt, the sons of President Teddy Roosevelt, shot a panda as it was sleepily coming out of a hollow tree and walking slowly into the bamboo. The panda was preserved by a taxidermist and exhibited in Chicago.

The first person to bring a living panda to the United States was a woman named Ruth Harkness. She was certainly not a typical hunter. She was a dress designer.

In 1934, her husband, William Harkness, had set out to capture a live panda for the Bronx Zoo. But he died in China before he even reached panda territory.

Ruth Harkness then did something that startled everyone. She left for China, determined to finish up the job her husband had wanted to do.

Reaching Shanghai, she teamed up with a young Chinese-American hunter named Quentin Young. They went 1,500 miles by boat, up the Yangtze River to Chunking. The last part of the trip was on foot. They climbed upward into the mountains. Reaching panda territory, they set up a base camp and put out foot traps of wire and rope, feeling this was the best way to capture a live panda. But that is not the way they finally got one.

As they went out to inspect the traps one day, sometimes moving through the thickets on hands and knees, Ruth Harkness heard a shot, then a yell. One of the guides had seen a panda and shot at it. Ruth Harkness was angry at this. She had given orders that there was to be no killing of pandas.

As they stood in a clearing, they heard a little cry coming from a hollow tree. Quentin Young went over to it and pulled something out. It was a baby panda, so small he could hold it in the palms of his hands.

Back at base camp, they fed it from a bottle and named it Su-Lin, which means "a little bit of something cute." In December, Mrs. Harkness sailed back to the United States carrying Su-Lin in a little wicker basket. Three months later, she left Su-Lin at the Brookfield Zoo in Chicago. That night, she woke up at midnight. That was the time she used to feed the baby panda every night. When she realized that Su-Lin was no longer with her, she wept. She missed that "little bit of something cute."

39

Ruth Harkness and Su-lin.

Su-Lin lived at the zoo about fourteen months, then died of a freak accident. A piece of wood got stuck in her throat, and she choked to death.

Su-Lin was important in several ways. She was the first living panda ever to reach the Western world. Also, she helped to change people's feelings about shooting pandas. After holding the cub in his arms, one of the big game hunters had said, "Mrs. Harkness, I'd never be able to shoot another panda."

Pandora at the Bronx Zoo.

SEVEN

FAMOUS ZOO PANDAS

SUDDENLY A REAL rush was on for living pandas. Every zoo wanted one. Pandora the panda arrived at the Bronx Zoo in New York in 1938. Like Su-Lin, she was an instant hit. She was a young, 24-pound cub when she arrived, cuddly, small and playful. Huge crowds came to see her as she tried to sit on a rubber ball and slipped and slid on the plank leading up to her sleeping platform, where she slept on a bed of shredded sugar cane.

Pandora got here just in time for the New York World's Fair of 1939, where she was shown in a special, glass-fronted air-conditioned enclosure. At the fair, she was just as popular as she was at the zoo. After watching her for a long time as she played, bumbled around and acted like a clown, a man said: "That's no animal. That's a man dressed up in some kind of a skin." He thought the things she did were too funny to be just accidental.

"Look," he added, "you can't tell me that a dumb

animal watches a crowd and knows what makes them laugh, and then does it again to get another laugh!"

There was a professional hunter named Tangier Smith who sometimes called himself by another name—"Zoology Jones." Smith—or Jones—led the most successful expedition of all, bringing back six pandas. He must have just seen the movie *Snow White and the Seven Dwarfs*, because he named three of his pandas Grumpy, Dopey and Happy. But it was one of the others, whom he named Baby, who became the best known.

Baby was sold to the Regent's Park Zoo in London, where they renamed her Ming. Like Su-Lin and Pandora, Ming was jolly and playful. In the spring of 1939, Ming was even visited by the royal family, and Queen Mary had a good laugh when Ming made a grab for her umbrella. She laughed even more when Ming seemed to giggle as she was being tickled on the stomach.

But the happy times were about to come to an end. Several months later, World War II began. Now Ming seemed especially important, since she gave so much pleasure to the British people at war and the thousands of soldiers on leave, who came to see her to get a good laugh.

But the war did not agree with Ming any more than it does with people. In 1940, the "blitz" began. For eight months straight, every single night, London was bombed by German planes. The once-playful Ming was upset by the sound of the falling bombs. Her hair fell out, and she became mangy. Often she just sat in her cage with her paws held over her eyes. In 1944, Ming died.

By the late 1930s, eleven living pandas had been taken out of China. Also, some expeditions had shot several more. Eleven plus a few more does not seem like a large number. But the panda was a rare animal. There were not many of them living up there in the bamboo mountain territory. If the hunting and trapping were to keep on, possibly soon there would be no more pandas left at all.

For this reason, in 1939, China passed a new law. No more pandas were allowed to be taken out of China. After this, for a long time, only a few pandas left China. And these were very special cases.

During this time, war was causing great suffering for the people of China, which had been invaded by Japan.* Cities and countryside were being bombed. There were food shortages and illness, as well as the problem of taking care of the wounded. To help lessen the suffering, the United States sent food and medical supplies to China through the United China Relief.

The Chinese knew how much the Americans had loved

---

* Later on, along with the United States, Britain, Russia and the other allied nations, China would be fighting against the Axis countries—Germany and Italy as well as Japan.

45

Pandora, who had since died. And so, even though there was a ban on exporting pandas, Madame Chiang Kai Shek and her sister, Madame Hong, arranged for the Bronx Zoo to be presented with another panda. It would, she said, be a gift to the children of America. It was a way of saying "thank you" from the Chinese people for the help they had received from the United China Relief.

John Tee Van of the Bronx Zoo went to China to collect the panda. When he got there, to his delight he found they had not one but two pandas to give him. He and the two pandas left China in a wartime blacked-out plane. Landing in the Philippines, they then set sail across the Pacific. But while they were at sea, Japan attacked Pearl Harbor in Hawaii on December 7, 1941, and the United States was soon at war with Japan. This meant that the ship carrying the two pandas was now traveling over seas filled with enemy ships and submarines, liable to attack at any time. Fortunately, they made it safely to Hawaii, then to San Francisco and across the United States to the Bronx Zoo. There, the two pandas, which had been named Pan-dee and Pan-duh began to amuse visitors with the usual panda shenanigans. First, Pan-dee climbed a tree forty feet high (about 12 meters) and stayed up there for forty-one hours. Then, at their birthday party, Pan-duh sat right on their birthday cake, while Pan-dee, joining in the fun, overturned all the chairs.

Only one more special panda was allowed to leave China in the 'forties. In 1946, after the war, it was ar-

Pan-dee and Pan-duh.

ranged that another panda was to be given to England by China as a bond of friendship between the two countries.

It took 200 hunters two months of searching and tracking to get this panda. When their dogs went after her, she climbed a tree. They tried to lasso her to get her down. But each time they threw the lasso, the panda caught the rope and pushed it off her body. After many throws, they finally got her and forced her down.

She was given the name Lien-Ho, which means "Unity."

Lien-Ho soon lost her fear of humans. She seemed relaxed and ate honey and bamboo. She was put in a crate and began her flight to London. When they landed in Calcutta, India, it was almost 100° Fahrenheit (37° Celsius) in the shade. Lien-Ho, accustomed to a cold, damp climate, did not seem well. A cold storage and ice factory came to the rescue. They agreed to let her stay in their plant while in Calcutta.

Once again on the plane, she was panting and looked sick. Dr. Ma Teh, who had led her capture and was now escorting her to England, was prepared. He had big slabs of ice, which they put in the panda's compartment. Soon she was happily rolling about on top of them.

When Lien Ho got to the zoo in London, she seemed miserable. She was not playful, like Ming. All she seemed to want to do was to sit around or sleep. She preferred to stay in the quiet darkness of the rear of her den. The only way they could get her out where people could see her was to lay a path of bamboo leading out.

One day Lien-Ho livened things up by breaking down a gate and escaping from her enclosure. She ended up in the nurse's hut, where the frightened nurse prepared to protect herself with a broom. But Lien Ho ignored the nurse and just sniffed around the piles of bandages until she was taken back to her enclosure.

During her four years at the zoo, Lien-Ho certainly seemed to be a sad animal.

"Are we really a civilized nation," someone wrote in a newspaper, "when we hunt this little wild creature, the panda, take away its freedom and force it to be stared at in the zoo, though it is so obviously thoroughly bewildered and unhappy?"

Author's Note: Since, during their lifetimes, Su-Lin and Lien-Ho were thought to be females, and Pan-duh was thought to be a male, that is how I have referred to them in this chapter. However, after their deaths, when autopsies were performed, it was discovered that Su-Lin and Lien-Ho were both really males; Pan-duh was really a female. It was easy for zoo people to make this sort of mistake.

The sex organs of pandas are very small, and until a panda is about six years old, it is very difficult to tell whether it is a male or a female—and even after that age, it is hard because the sex organs of both males and females are covered by layers of fat.

49

EIGHT

YOU BE THE SCIENTIST

～

THE PANDA was not always known by the name "panda."

The Chinese had always thought it was a kind of bear. Sometimes they called it the clawed bear or the bamboo bear. Other names for it were the harlequin bear, the speckled bear, and the cat-bear. Most often, it was called "bei-shung"—the white bear.

Is the panda a kind of bear?

In size and shape, it looks a lot like a bear. It climbs trees like a bear. And it moves and sits in a bearlike way. There is another way it resembles a bear. Its young are unusually small at birth as compared to the size of an adult. A mother grizzly bear may weigh 500 pounds (226 kilograms). Her newborn cub weighs about a pound (less than half a kilogram).

When Père David discovered the panda in 1879, he

50

also thought it was some kind of bear. Since the person who discovers a new species has the honor of naming it, Père David gave it the name *Ursus melanoleucus*. This means, in Latin, "black and white bear."

Excited by his discovery, he sent a specimen of the animal—a skin and skeleton—to his friend, Professor Alphonse Milne-Edwards, in Paris. There, at the natural history museum, the new specimen was eagerly examined. Soon they saw things that made them disagree with Père David. They did not think the animal was a bear.

When scientists try and decide which animals are in the same "family" and are most closely related to each other, they don't just go by what the animal looks like, or

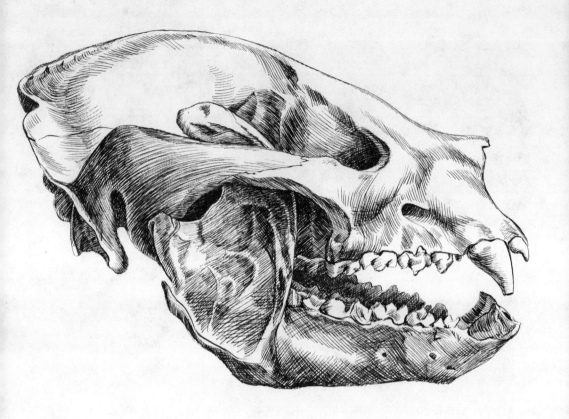

Panda skull

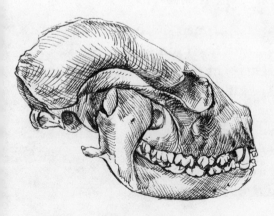

Red panda skull

Bear skull

by its behavior. There are other things they consider more basic. A similarity in the bone structure is considered important, especially foot and leg bones. Teeth and skull are also important. (Thus, for example, the hippo is considered more closely related to the giraffe than it is to the rhino, even though a hippo and rhino *look* more alike.)

Examining the remains of the panda, this is what Milne-Edwards and the others saw:

The skull did not resemble that of a bear. It was different in shape; shorter in the muzzle, and also heavier and more solid than a bear skull.

The jaws and teeth were not like those of a bear, either.

The red panda is in the raccoon family.

Nor were the feet and legs. The skeleton in general was not really bearlike.

Then, examining the foot and leg bones more carefully, they saw the most telling feature of all—that extension of the wristbone, creating the unusual sixth claw, or "panda's thumb."

No bear has anything like that. But they knew another animal that did; it was called the red panda. It was a small animal with reddish fur, a bushy, ringed tail and a fox-like white face. It was in the raccoon family. Its scientific name was *Ailurus fulgens*, meaning "fire-colored cat."

Certainly Père David's animal and the red panda did not *look* alike. One was large and bearlike, the other small and raccoonlike. But they did have other important things in common. Their skulls were both short-muzzled and similar in shape. Their jaws and teeth were also quite similar. They were alike in another curious way: they both ate bamboo. (Panda is a Nepalese word meaning "bamboo-eater.")

As the scientists examined Père David's new specimen, they became more and more convinced that these two animals were closely related. If so, since the red panda was in the raccoon family, they felt the newly discovered animal must also be in the raccoon family. It was not a bear at all!

This meant it could not keep the name *Ursus* (bear) given to it by Père David. Its name was changed to *Ailuropoda melanoleucus*—meaning "black and white cat-foot."

As time went on, the larger panda was known as the Great Panda, and the small, fire-colored one called the Lesser Panda. We now call the large one the Giant Panda.

But the change in name did not settle the argument. Through the years, many scientists have felt that Père David *was* right, and that the giant panda does belong in the bear family. In their view, the fact that both kinds of pandas have the "panda's thumb" doesn't prove the giant panda is in the raccoon family, or even that the two animals are closely related. They feel that the red panda and the giant panda may simply have developed this unusual feature independently.

They feel the similarity in the two animals' teeth doesn't prove a close relationship, either. It is possible,

Is the panda a close relation of the bear . . . or the raccoon . . . or neither one?

they say, that both animals developed the same type of teeth because they both eat the same diet—bamboo.

They feel the two pandas are not in the same family, but belong in two different families: the giant panda in the bear family, and the lesser panda in the raccoon family.

New lab techniques developed in recent years have provided evidence for both sides of the panda argument. Blood can now be analyzed. The blood of the giant panda has been found to be more like bear blood than red panda blood.

That doesn't prove anything, say the people who believe the giant panda is a member of the raccoon family, because they have another new fact on *their* side. The giant panda has the same number of chromosomes as the raccoon (42). Different kinds of bears have been shown to have either 56 or 74 chromosomes.

Chromosomes are that part of the cell that carry the genes, which determine an animal's qualities. So this would seem to be an important point. We also know the stomach, liver and intestines of the giant panda are more like that of a raccoon than that of a bear.

So, although the giant panda was discovered more than 100 years ago, the argument about it is still going on:

Is the giant panda a super-huge raccoon-type animal? Or is it a rather unusual bear-type animal?

George Schaller and many Chinese scientists do not

agree with either side. They have a different point of view altogether. A giant panda is not a raccoon, they say. And it is not a bear. They feel the panda is a sufficiently different kind of animal to be in a family of its own. "A panda is a panda," says George Schaller.

What do *you* think? *You* be the scientist.

Think of all the important points. List them. Maybe it would help you to do some extra reading about bears and about raccoons. You may also want to read a little about animal classification. (This is our system of placing animals in different "families" and other groupings.) Then try to come to your own conclusion.

Do you think the panda belongs in the bear family, or in the racoon family? Or do you think the giant panda is an animal special enough to be in a family of its own?

NINE

DANGER TO THE PANDA!

WHEN WORLD WAR II was over, the new Chinese govern-ment—the People's Republic of China—turned its atten-tion to its wildlife. The Chinese were proud of the interesting animals living in their country, and wished to protect them. They set aside huge areas—millions of acres—as natural reserves, where wildlife could live, safe and protected.

They were especially concerned about the pandas. Pandas lived in several different areas of the Szechuan Province in the central part of China. All of these areas were made into natural reserves. It was illegal for anyone to hunt pandas, or disturb them in any way.

This did not mean that people outside of China would never again have the chance to see a panda. There was now another way for zoos to get these animals. Often the Chinese government would give a pair of pandas to another country as a gift of friendship. Hsing-Hsing and

Ling-Ling came here in this way. They were a gift from China to the American people after President Nixon's visit to China in 1972. Zoos in Britain, Japan, France, Russia, Spain, Germany and Mexico have also received pandas as gifts.

How many pandas still existed in the wild? No one really knew. So, in the 1970s, a "panda census" was made. Thousands of people worked on it. Going through the forests, they tried to count all the pandas they saw. As you can imagine, it would be hard to get an exact number this way. But when they finished, they estimated that at most there were about 1,000 pandas. Not any more—and possibly many fewer.

Pandas have natural enemies. There are predators, such as leopards and the wild dogs that hunt in packs, roaming the mountainsides. But adult pandas can defend themselves, and often kill or inflict bad wounds on an attacker. And so the predators normally do not attack an adult panda.

A thousand pandas or fewer is not a large number in terms of a total animal population. But with their huge reserves to live on, protection against hunters, and their ability to defend themselves against predators, it was thought the pandas were safe and would have no problem surviving.

We know now we were wrong. Suddenly, in the winter of 1975–76, a large number of pandas died. They died because of a "bamboo failure."

*

One of the unusual things about bamboo is that it blooms and comes into flower only at very long intervals. Some types bloom only every 100 years. After it blooms, every plant of that species dies. Until new shoots grow from the seeds, there are none growing.

A type of bamboo called "umbrella bamboo" grows over 2,000 square miles (about 5,180 square kilometers) of mountainside. In the winter of 1975–76, it flowered, then died, Suddenly, in this tremendous area, there was no food for the pandas.

In past times when this happened, the pandas would descend to lower slopes where other species of bamboo were still growing. But this time, when the pandas, desperate for food, came down to the lower slopes, there *was* no bamboo growing there. It had been cut down. The land had been cleared to make room for farms. Instead of finding bamboo, the pandas found only cultivated fields.

When pandas began appearing in the fields and eating wheat and corn, the local farmers knew something was wrong. They had never seen pandas do this before. They quickly notified the authorities. People were sent up into the mountains with ropes and nets to try and capture all the starving pandas they could find. They carried them down to the villages and fed them sweet potatoes and cereal. Not many pandas could be saved, though; they were already too sick and weak.

That year, the bodies of 138 pandas were found. It is impossible to know how many more died and were never found.

Desperate for food, the pandas come down to the lower slopes.

Soon there was even more bad news. Within the next ten years, another bamboo species was expected to have a "die-off."

The Chinese government did whatever it could to help the remaining pandas. The panda reserves were made larger. Soon the ten special panda reserves covered almost one and a half million acres. Even more important, no more bamboo cutting was allowed within these areas.

Then Chinese officials met with Peter Scott, head of the World Wildlife Fund, and other Western scientists. Together they planned on what they could do to help save the pandas.

The meeting was held at the Wolong Natural Reserve, the largest of the panda reserves, which covers about 800 square miles (about 2,072 square kilometers), although only about a fifth of it, the higher sections, is inhabited by pandas.

It was here that they would concentrate their efforts. The cost of the project was figured to be 4.5 million dollars, with China providing 3.5 million and the World Wildlife Fund the remaining million.

The project got under way quickly. First they set up a research station where pandas are held and studied. The pandas here have large natural outdoor areas where they can roam about and climb trees.

There is a breeding station, too, where they have pairs of pandas they hope will mate and have young. Dr. Devra Kleiman of the National Zoo in Washington and Dr. Emil Dolensek of the Bronx Zoo have been active in this project. There are also biologists at Wolong, studying the

64

The research station at Wolong.

bamboo. The entire panda project is a cooperative effort, with experts from different countries working together. Everything they learn they share with professors, students, game wardens, and anyone else involved with pandas.

And they also made plans for the next bamboo die-off. The next time another kind of bamboo flowers and dies, people would go high in the mountains and capture every panda they can. They would take them down to a special holding station, where the animals would be fed during the emergency. Then, when the new bamboo has grown, the pandas would be freed.

It has already happened and it is even worse than ex-

pected. In 1983, not one but two species of bamboo flowered. This meant the next die-off was starting. Mountainsides that had been covered with arrow and fountain bamboo were soon covered with dry, dead stems. In the Wolong area, where about 200 pandas live, it is especially bad. There, 90 percent of the bamboo is in various stages of dying. All through the panda habitat there will be a shortage of bamboo. The pandas are in their worst crisis ever.

An emergency plan was immediately put into action by the Chinese government.

It is early 1984. Rescue teams of four to six people living in small mountain huts are roaming the mountainsides, searching for starving pandas. When they find one, it is fed sugarcane, corn and meat, then put into a lightweight cage and carried down over the rugged terrain to the holding station below. Here it will be kept for several years till the bamboo forests have regrown. Then it will be released.

Food drops by air have been made. People in local villages are setting out food for any pandas that may wander down from nearby slopes. Food is also being placed up on higher slopes where the pandas wander. But pandas weakened by hunger do not wander as much as usual, and so there is no guarantee the starving pandas will find this food.

Some pandas will be trapped, IDs put on their ears and then they will be taken out and freed in areas where there are different species of bamboo growing.

The government has offered a reward of $100 (which equals about two months earnings for local Chinese) to anyone who reports and helps rescue a panda.

Considering the rugged terrain, the solitary habits of pandas, and the vast forest areas where they roam, the problems are immense. By spring, twelve pandas were rescued. Three others were found dead.

What will happen to Zhen-Zhen, Long-Long and Ning-Ning? Because they are being tracked and their locations are known and their activities monitored, the researchers will probably be able to tell if they are in trouble. So they have a much better chance of being saved than the others in remote areas whose locations are unknown. Still, there are no guarantees.

What will happen when this crisis is over? How many pandas will be left? And is there some way they will be able to survive on their own, without being rescued each time there is a new bamboo failure?

A world without animals would be a less interesting place for all of us . . .

TEN

THE FUTURE
OF THE PANDAS

‿‿

WHAT IS the future of the panda? Will we be able to keep it from becoming extinct?

Some animals that are extinct in the wild can keep on surviving in zoos. Père David's Deer—a type of deer discovered by Père David and named after him—has been extinct in the wild for about three thousand years. Yet herds of them are still alive in game parks and zoos. The ones Père David discovered in 1865 were living in captivity in the Imperial Gardens in Beijing (Peking). Now there are Père David's Deer in the Bronx Zoo, in Chicago, in Washington, D.C., San Antonio, and other zoos in different countries.

But it is not likely we could do this with the panda. Pandas have always been difficult to keep in captivity. With many of the early pandas, zoo life seemed to have affected their nervous system. Ming, Lien-Ho, Pandora and others died in this way. At the end of her life, Ming kept falling off her feet. Her body shook with epileptic convulsions that got worse and worse until she died.

This has not been happening to zoo pandas recently. Still, they need a lot of special care.

Also, it has always been difficult for pandas to breed in captivity. Until 1963, no panda had ever been born in a zoo. Then finally, in that year, one was born at the zoo in Beijing (Peking), China—a five-ounce healthy male cub, which they named Ming, meaning "brilliant."

Since then, more than 30 pandas have been born in zoos in China. But until recently, none had ever been born outside of China.

Then in August, 1980, there was exciting news from Mexico. At the Chapultepec Zoo in Mexico City, a baby panda was born—the first ever to be born outside of China!

Ying-Ying, the mother, nursed the cub and handled it gently. But seven days later, a tragedy occurred. Ying-Ying, in rolling over, accidentally crushed her tiny cub. When the keeper picked up and took away the dead baby panda, tears were rolling down Ying-Ying's face, and for two days, she would not eat or sleep.

Dr. Juan Giron Tellez has been taking care of the Mexican pandas since they arrived there in 1975. He feels the accident happened because Ying-Ying was made nervous by all the reporters and photographers taking pictures directly through a window.

The following year, Ying-Ying had another baby. This time, no direct viewing was allowed; reporters could see the pandas only on a TV monitor. The cub, named Tohui,

is doing fine, and is now several years old. And in the summer of 1983 another baby panda was born in Mexico!

Why has there been such success in Mexico, when elsewhere, apart from China, zoo pandas cannot seem to be able to breed?

Does it have to do with the fact that Pe-Pe and Ying-Ying were kept together since they arrived at the zoo as cubs? At other zoos, panda pairs are usually kept separated, except at breeding time. But since Pe-Pe and Ying-Ying enjoyed each other's company, they had been kept together. (After Tohui's birth, Pe-Pe began to fight, so now the three pandas are kept in separate enclosures.)

Could it possibly have anything to do with the fact that Mexico City is at an altitude of about 7,500 feet above sea level—more or less the same altitude at which pandas live in the wild?

Or, was it simply unusual good fortune?

With pandas, both the male *and* the female must be ready to breed at the same time. (With most other animals, only the female must be "ready.") Was it by chance that Pe-Pe and Ying-Ying's bodies have been "in tune" in this way?

The Mexican pandas are fed a diet of rice, milk, chicken, meat, carrots, apples, spinach, salt, sugar, vitamins, minerals, calcium and, of course, bamboo. They are healthy animals and have shown no signs of any disease of the nervous system that affected some of the early pandas.

Since pandas are accustomed to a cold, damp climate, their inside quarters have air-conditioning and humidifiers. Because it is hot in Mexico, they spend only the cooler times of day—early morning and late afternoon— in their larger, outdoor enclosures. Watching Pe-Pe outside one afternoon, several times I saw him come to the rear of the enclosure and stand at the wall that separated

Pe-Pe is now in a separate enclosure.

him from Ying-Ying. Was he lonesome? Did he know she was behind that wall?

In July, 1983, at the National Zoo in Washington, D.C., there was more news. A baby panda had finally been born to Ling-Ling and Hsing-Hsing. The zoo had been hoping for this for several years. And now it had happened. This was the first baby panda ever born in the United States.

Ling-Ling gently picked up her baby with her mouth and held it against her. But soon there was sad news. The baby panda died after only three hours. When its body was examined, it was found to have fluid in its lungs from a bacterial infection it had gotten shortly before birth.

Spring, 1984: At the National Zoo in Washington, Ling-Ling and Hsing-Hsing have again mated. Will Ling-Ling give birth to a cub? Even before they are sure this will happen, preparations are being made. In the woods in Pennsylvania, Gary Alt, a biologist and bear expert, is tranquilizing, then milking, female bears. The milk he obtains is sent to Washington. There, by analyzing it, Dr. Olav Oftedal, Head Nutritionist at the zoo, will be able to create a natural formula similar to panda milk.

If Ling-Ling gives birth, and for some reason does not nurse the cub, this formula will be used to feed it. If two cubs should happen to be born, and Ling-Ling is not able to nurse them both, the second cub will be taken and hand-reared and fed the special formula.

Zoo births are important. It is a way we can have pandas in zoos without having to take them out of the wild. But so far the answer to panda survival is clearly not in zoos. If pandas are to have any real chance of surviving, it must be

74

Pe-Pe is waiting to go inside.

in the wild. It is far better not to remove them from their natural habitat, but to leave them there undisturbed, to live and reproduce. Otherwise it is likely that soon there will be no pandas left in the world at all.

In the wild, there are possible ways we can help them. The problems of pandas are complicated because of the strange life cycle of bamboo and the way it "fails." Living in a large protected reserve is of no help to the pandas if they have no food to eat during a bamboo failure.

Perhaps farmers and villagers living on lower slopes of the panda's habitat could be relocated, and bamboo replanted where it had once grown—so that when the umbrella, arrow or fountain bamboo (the three species of bamboo that grow on the higher slopes) fail in the future, the pandas will once again be able to come down to lower slopes, as they did in past times, and find different kinds of bamboo available.

Would the Chinese be willing to do this?

One definite plan the Chinese have is to plant additional types of bamboo, so that with their different life cycles they will not all die out at once. Can it be done in time? Will it work?

Perhaps the research being done at Wolong will discover other ways to help the pandas.

Long ago, Père David wrote in his diary: "I passionately love the beauties of nature. The marvels of the hand of God transport me with such admiration that in comparison the finest work of man seems only trivial."

76

Ling-Ling.

Yet, some people are now saying: "Wild animals need too much space to live in. This is land that people could use. What is the difference," they say, "if some strange animal that lives far away disappears from the earth forever?"

But why must it be *either* people *or* animals that we care about? Isn't it an amazing thing that so many different kinds of animals can exist on earth? Shouldn't we work to find some way to be able to share the earth's space with all these wonderful creatures and do everything we can to keep them from becoming extinct? Animals are very special, and a world without them would be a much less interesting place for all of us.

Meanwhile, in China, Project Panda Watch is still going on. They've learned a lot about pandas that no one ever knew before. Some of the new things learned about pandas' needs and behavior may help us to help them survive.

BIBLIOGRAPHY

Bridges, William. *Zoology Goes to the World's Fair of 1939.* Bulletin of New York Zoological Society, May–June, 1941.

Carter, T. Donald. *The Giant Panda.* Bulletin of New York Zoological Society, Jan.–Feb., 1937.

Chorn, John and Hoffman, Robert S. *Mammalian Species #110.* American Society of Mammalogists, December, 1978.

Graham, David Crocket. *How the Baby Pandas Were Captured.* Bulletin of New York Zoological Society, Jan.–Feb., 1942.

Grzimek, Dr. H. C. Bernhard, ed. *Grzimek's Animal Life Encyclopedia.* New York, Van Nostrand Reinhold Co., 1975.

Immelmann, Klaus, ed. *Grzimek's Encyclopedia of Ethology.* New York, Van Nostrand Reinhold Co., 1977.

Marden, Luis. "Bamboo, The Giant Grass." *National Geographic,* October, 1980.

Morris, Ramona and Desmond. *The Giant Panda*. Harmondsworth and New York, Penguin Books, 1982.

Muller-Schwarze, Dietland and Silverstein, Robert M. *Chemical Signals in Vertebrates 3*. New York and London, Plenum Press, 1983.

Reed, Theodore H. "What's Black and White and Loved All Over?" *National Geographic*, December, 1972.

Sage, Dean. *How Pandora Came to the Zoological Park*. Bulletin of New York Zoological Society, July–Aug., 1938.

Schaller, George B. "Pandas in the Wild." *National Geographic*, December, 1981.

———. "Zhen-Zhen, Rare Treasure of Sichuan." *Animal Kingdom*, December, 1982–January, 1983.

Tee Van, John. *Two Pandas; China's Gift to America*. Bulletin of New York Zoological Society, Jan.–Feb., 1942.

Zhu Jing and Li Yangwen. *The Giant Panda*. Beijing, China, Science Press, 1980. Distributed in U.S. by Van Nostrand Reinhold.

Save the Panda. A *National Geographic* TV Special, televised March 9, 1983.

GLOSSARY

carnivore: any of the animals in the order, or group, of meat-eating mammals called carnivores. Some carnivores eat both meat and plant foods.

conservation: preserving; saving and protecting something.

convulsion: involuntary contraction of the muscles, causing shaking or twitching movements.

epileptic: relating to the disease called epilepsy, which affects the nervous system.

esophagus: a muscular tube in the body through which food goes down to the stomach.

extinct: no longer existing, and with no possibility of ever existing in the future.

family: a group of animals (or plants) that have some basic physical characteristics in common and are thus considered closely related to one another.

goral: a goatlike, mountain-dwelling horned, hoofed mammal; its weight is about 60 pounds.

gut: the intestines—the tube-like passageway going through the body in which food is digested and absorbed.

herbivore: an animal that mainly eats plant foods.

hypodermic: used to inject something beneath the skin.

intestines: the tube-like passageway going through the body where food is digested and absorbed; it goes from the stomach to the anus.

mangy: having loss of hair.

muntjac: a small slender deer weighing about 30 pounds; it barks if alarmed and is therefore known as "the barking deer."

predator: a meat-eating animal that hunts and kills for food.

radio collar: a collar fitted with radio equipment which indicates the distance away of the animal wearing the collar.

radiotelemetry: measuring the distance of an object by means of radio waves.

research: investigation for the purpose of discovery of facts.

serow: a sure-footed horned, hoofed mammal; is dark-furred and lives on high, rocky ridges: weighs about 150 pounds.

shrew: a tiny mouse-like animal with a long, pointy nose.

species: a group of individuals that are alike in all basic physical characteristics. Individuals within a species can breed and bear young of their kind.

takin: a mountain-dwelling horned, hoofed mammal; brownish or golden colored, heavily built; weighs about 500 pounds.

taxidermist: one who does taxidermy—a technique by which dead animals are treated and preserved.

vole: a small rodent resembling a mouse.

zoology: the study of animal life.

INDEX

INDEX